JIM GEARS

AMAZING GUIDES TO TINY HOMES

By Jim Gears

Copyright © 2017 by Jim Gears

All Rights Reserved. This document is geared towards providing exact and reliable information in regards to the topic and issue covered. The publication is sold with the idea that the publisher is not required to render accounting, officially permitted, or otherwise, qualified services. If advice is necessary, legal or professional, a practiced individual in the profession should be ordered.

- From a Declaration of Principles which was accepted and approved equally by a Committee of the American Bar Association and a Committee of Publishers and Associations.

In no way is it legal to reproduce, duplicate, or transmit any part of this document in either electronic means or in printed format. Recording of this publication is strictly prohibited and any storage of this document is not allowed unless with written permission from the publisher. All rights reserved.

The information provided herein is stated to be truthful and consistent, in that any liability, in terms of inattention or otherwise, by any usage or abuse of any policies, processes, or directions contained within is the solitary and utter responsibility of the recipient reader. Under no circumstances will any legal responsibility or blame be held against the publisher for any reparation, damages, or monetary loss due to the information herein, either directly or indirectly.

Respective authors own all copyrights not held by the publisher.

The information herein is offered for informational purposes solely, and is universal as so. The presentation of the information is without contract or any type of guarantee assurance.

The trademarks that are used are without any consent, and the publication of the trademark is without permission or backing by the trademark owner. All trademarks and brands within this book are for clarifying purposes only and are the owned by the owners themselves, not affiliated with this document.

Disclaimer and Terms of Use: The Author and Publisher has strived to be as accurate and complete as possible in the creation of this book, notwithstanding the fact that he does not warrant or represent at any time that the contents within are accurate due to the rapidly changing nature of the Internet. While all attempts have been made to verify information provided in this publication, the Author and Publisher assumes no responsibility for errors, omissions, or contrary interpretation of the subject matter herein.

Any perceived slights of specific persons, peoples, or organizations are unintentional. In practical advice books, like anything else in life, there are no guarantees of results. Readers are cautioned to rely on their own judgment about their individual circumstances and act accordingly.

This book is not intended for use as a source of legal, medical, business, accounting or financial advice. All readers are advised to seek services of competent professionals in the legal, medical, business, accounting, and finance fields.

TABLE OF CONTENTS

Introduction 5

Chapter 1
Origins Of The Tiny House 7

Chapter 2
Is Tiny House Living For You? 9

Chapter 3
To Build Or To Buy 12

Chapter 4
Guide To Building A Tiny House 18

Chapter 5
How To Buy A Tiny House 26

Chapter 6
Space Saving Hacks And Furniture 31

Chapter 7
Things To Consider When Buying Tiny House Kits 34

Chapter 8
Tiny House Plans 36

Chapter 9
Tiny Homes Faqs 39

Chapter 10
How To Make It Big With Tiny House Kits 41

Chapter 11
The Advantages Of Living In Tiny Houses 43

Conclusion 46

INTRODUCTION

Tiny houses serve as a renewed concept in real estate. After decades of building bigger and bigger homes, a few people are recognizing the impact of large houses on the environment. Instead, they are opting for these miniature homes that provide much needed freedom.

Now there are companies that build these homes, sell floor plans, rent or sell them. Despite the similarity to RV or camper, these homes offer an alternative living style.

With a size under 500 square feet, it's not a lifestyle accepted by the majority, but the popularity is rising. As a form of permanent residence, these tiny homes have their own unique set of benefits and challenges.

First and foremost, smaller homes offer financial freedom that most Americans could only dream of. Image a life without worrying about mortgage payments. What would you do with that extra money? Image not having to work so hard to pay the mortgage, what would you do with your time?

These tiny houses also have much smaller utility bills. Some of these homes have plumbing and electricity just like a regular house, only on a much smaller scale that leads to much smaller utility bills. The more eco-conscious residents may install a solar panel and use propane for heat during the winter.

Some choose to use composting toilets that turns human excretion into compost. In this case, no septic system is necessary.

There is also geographical freedom. Considering how many people make long commutes daily because the sizable home they can afford is so far away, small homes present the geographic flexibility as they take up so little land. Previous research evidence showed there was a link between long commute and poor health.

Those who drive long distances to work tend to be less physically active and suffer from hypertension. Tiny homes are easy to move as the owner relocates, saving relocation expenses.

Smaller residence also forces the owner to expand their living area onto a deck, garden, and surrounding area. This works for those loving the outdoors and connecting with nature.

What attracts people to a small home is more than its size; it's the lifestyle behind it. Limited space forces people to cut down on unnecessary possessions. In the land of excess, most people own way more than they need. When designed efficiently, these tiny homes can serve all functions of regular sized homes.

There are plenty of challenges to living in a house the size of a walk-in closet. Small space can easily get cluttered if one gets away from the minimalist mindset. It also may lead to cabin fever during days of inclement weather.

Not all neighborhoods welcome miniature houses. Some have building codes that specify a range of home sizes. Neighbors may despise them in fear of a drop in real estate value. On top of that, how different do you want to be from your friends or colleagues? Our residence is a display of our status, wealth, and success.

After all, it takes a special kind of mindset, personality, and motivation to choose tiny homes over gigantic mansions. On one hand, there's freedom from financial and geographical restraints. On the other hand, there's a great social norm to conform to in order to fit in.

Learn more about tiny homes in this AMAZING GUIDE.

CHAPTER I
ORIGINS OF THE TINY HOUSE

Mr. Jay Shafer is the responsible genius that came up with the idea of Tiny Houses! His company, known as Tumbleweed, is part of the small house movement. In 2002, He co-founded the Small House Society in Iowa City, Iowa.

In 2003 he was commissioned by Gregory Paul Johnson to build The Mobile Hermitage, which became one of Tumbleweed's first commercially sold homes.

WHEN DID TINY HOUSES BEGIN BLOOMING?

Turns out to be that during the Katrina Hurricane disaster in 2005, Marianne Cusato developed 308 sq. ft. cottage constructions for the homeless victims and the small house movements bloomed.

If you want a tiny house, Identify the square footage you will need. Visit local pre-fab buildings to get the feel of what's your minimum requirement or rent out a Tiny House for a week-end to make an assessment and experience your hands-on living inside a Tiny House.

Then start brainstorming and planning the set-up and your storage needs. Slowly, but surely you will start forming your image of the inside of your Tiny House.

A pre-fab building of 320 sq. ft. is quite enough to make it comfortable and the transition from big to small very easy. Some even include all appliances and HVAC systems. All you need to do is pay for the building plus taxes and transportation. Another alternative is to contact a builder of your choice.

You also need to research the State laws and requirements for these Tiny Houses. There are several different resources and websites that sell plans, workshops, existing real estate for sale or even rentals. So these small homes are here to stay for a long time and a definite solution for not paying mortgage for 30 or 40 years.

Picture yourself inside a Tiny House and exactly what you expect in order to feel and be comfortable. Let's entertain our thoughts right now... think of having enough kitchen cabinets, maybe a slide-out pantry, a small range with oven, enough counter space for preparing foods, a small sink, closets for your bedroom, and where would you squeeze in your washer/dryer combo, oh... and don't forget of your bathroom commodities.

Do you want a loft or same floor bedroom? If you have a loft, how will you want your stairway? Will you have storage underneath or within your stairway?

As for your living room area, get into creative gear for saving space with a small sofa with drawers or underneath storage, maybe a drop-leaf table for dining or working with a laptop and continue to work on all your ideas by jotting them down. Then with all your ideas prepare a layout drawing and include measurements.

There are many ideas out there for small scale furniture that save floor area. Sofas with storage drawers, corner desks, floating desks, drop leaf folding tables, storage trunks, Murphy beds, bed that slide out or up and down from the ceiling any many more.

CHAPTER 2
IS TINY HOUSE LIVING FOR YOU?

It seems this tiny trend is catching on all across the world. Individuals, couples and small families are choosing to downsize their lives to live in much smaller spaces that are usually much less expensive than conventional houses.

Small houses like this can range in size from less than 100 square feet to up to 900 hundred square feet. So, you're interested in knowing more about the Tiny House movement? Before going through the process of building or buying you own, this information can help you narrow down your small living choices.

Tiny Houses are often on wheels, but not always. One of the leaders of the small living movement, Jay Shafer of the Tumbleweed Tiny House Company, suggests building the little houses on trailers so they can be moved easily. This also helps get around some of the laws surrounding such small homes.

Many municipalities have codes that don't allow people to live in spaces under a certain square footage. By building a house on a trailer, it is no longer a house and it becomes an RV. Not everyone builds these small homes on wheels. Check your local codes to see if a small house might classify as a "building of no consequence" before starting your project

Tiny houses are often sustainable, but not always. The small home movement and environmentalism seem to go hand in hand. Many builders use sustainable building products and create environmentally friendly systems in their homes.

It is not unusual to find a small home built with all reclaimed wood. Sometimes it is difficult to build a conventional home using these items, but the scale these houses allows the builder to use much less of the product making it effectively cheaper. Many small homes are also off the grid using solar energy or rain catchment systems for water use.

Tiny houses are built with all the necessities of a conventional house. There will typically be a seating area, a dining area, a kitchen, a bathroom and a sleeping area which is most often a loft. The beauty about the tiny house movement is that the each owner and builder can customize the space to work best with their own lives.

HOW TO FIGURE THIS OUT?

Styrofoam sheets can be found at most retail stores for as low as $5 or $6. They come in different sizes and thickness, so thin foams would work as they are easy to cut and glue. With a ruler on hand, each inch could be the equivalent of 1 foot.

Get all your items spaced out where you would really place them in a real tiny house and then figure out how many feet long and wide do you need your home to be. Example: 8 ft. wide x 30 ft. long x 13.5 ft. high.

As you think about floor plans and where you would place your kitchen cabinets, appliances, pantry, closets, furniture, etc., keep in mind your wants as your needs for your small house living. Would or could you live inside a Tiny House 24/7? So now you have a better idea... got to have your wants as well as your needs. This is going to be a fun project to work on!

DOWNSIZING

Downsizing, after all, is a smart thing to do. It's hard to start, but once you do, you will find so many items you no longer use or need. All of those items can be donated to different entities such as, Salvation Army, Paralyzed Veterans, people who have lost their homes in fires or tornadoes. Other options are yard or garage sales.

You will find there are different stages in your life. When you're young and adventurous, mid-age saving mode, growing into the golden age and priorities have shifted into more practical solutions to just about everything in life.

So no matter what stage you identify yourself in, if you are considering to live inside a Tiny House, downsizing is a healthy decision both emotionally and economically.

CHAPTER 3
TO BUILD OR TO BUY

The tiny house movement emphasizes downsizing and living with just what you need. Many young people and retired couples see the advantages of avoiding mortgage payments and cutting loose by living tiny.

A few companies have tiny homes for sale, but many believers in the movement are building their own. Here are a few important factors in the choice of whether to build or buy.

CONSTRUCTION SKILLS

While most people can improvise a structure in the wilderness, the bamboo-and-leaf structures of LOST wouldn't be up to the building codes in most suburbs.

Not only are there some basic carpentry skills and a whole set of tools that become necessary, but would-be-builders should also consider the need for more complex skills involving electrician work and plumbing. The DIY route is appealing, but the average handyman is quickly out of his depth with this project.

SPECIALIZED MATERIALS

The amateur contractor may have some serious remodeling projects under his or her belt, but building a structure on a trailer requires special considerations for weight and durability.

The tiny homes for sale by professionals are built to handle travel at highway speeds, when a little wobble in the wind can torque the whole structure. Other residences may only experience comparable strain in an earthquake or hurricane, but many of the people who live in 100 square feet need to move the home every few years.

PROFESSIONAL WARRANTIES

Shopping for homes for sale will allow you to choose between different warranties. The structure you build yourself doesn't have a professional guarantee that it will stand up to weather, time, and adverse circumstances.

Contractors and turnkey builders have a range of options where your investment will be protected for months or years. Homeowners insurance isn't always available for these minuscule structures, and not all insurance providers would endorse the stability of a DIY structure.

POTENTIAL FOR RESELL

These little houses are not a popular investment for flippers because they don't tend to retain value well. Inhabited trailers have a similar problem, in that they are significantly less attractive after having been lived-in for years.

That said, buyers looking for a deal will be far more likely to consider paying for a getaway residence that has been assembled by people with know-how. Your considerable DIY skills are difficult for a third party to evaluate, and so purchasers will likely assume that the wiring and other key components will need a thorough inspection.

Living in a miniature, mobile space can be liberating for people with the right temperament. Unfortunately, not all of the people with the inclination towards that lifestyle can manage the complex set of challenges that come with construction.

The movement toward these structures is gathering steam, and increasing numbers of books and other resources are available. Those who are undecided about their abilities should invest time in watching instructional DIY videos and consider paying to visit a conference.

If possible, try contacting other people who have attempted the project, and see what you can learn.

Below is my list of the many benefits of owning a tiny home. Here we go...

LESS INITIAL COST

A tiny house is obviously smaller than a traditional home. There are less materials and the labor required to build it because of its size.

Since tiny homes often have most of the features a traditional house has (kitchen, plumbing, roof, and flooring) the price per square foot is usually more expensive. But since overall size of the house is so much smaller, the overall price is only a fraction of traditional homes.

LESS ENERGY CONSUMPTION

Tiny homes require much less energy to heat and cool simply because they have much less interior air space. Since many tiny homes are on wheels, a tiny house owner could move their house under a large tree in the summer, and out into the sun during the winter.

Two additional culprits for significant energy consumption are refrigerators and hot water heaters. Both are typically smaller in a tiny house and consume far less energy. Another use of energy is your own energy.

It doesn't take long to tidy up a very small dwelling. I have seen folks who have been very creative with reducing their tiny house's energy consumption and making use of the fact that their home is very small. Solar panels, wood stoves, wind turbines, compost toilets, the list goes on and on.

LESS WATER CONSUMPTION AND TRASH

If you have a small shower and small hot water heater, chances are your showers will be alot shorter. If you have a small trash can, chances are you will generate less trash. Using less water and producing less trash is both good for environment and your wallet.

LESS COST FOR REPAIRS

Repair costs for your tiny home are simply a matter of mathematics. The cost to replace the roof of a 2,000 square foot home will be a lot less than the cost of a 300 square foot home. This is of course because of the reduction in materials and labor.

LESS LAND TO PURCHASE AND UPKEEP

A small dwelling will require less land reside on. Since many cities have restrictions on the size a home can be, you may be required to purchase land outside the city with no restrictions. Land outside the city is cheaper to purchase and the taxes are less.

If you elect to buy a very small plot of land that your house will reside on, you'll spend less time cutting grass. If you buy a regular sized lot, you'll have more room your garden.

LESS FOOD

If you have a small pantry, you'll have a small amount of food in your house. If you can look through your kitchen window and see fresh vegetables growing in it, you'll spend less produce. By eating less food in your tiny house, you'll keep your food bill and weight down.

LESS TAXES

Since the value of your tiny home and land is resides on is less valuable (assuming you choose to buy your land rather than lease) your tax bill will be less. The savings can go towards investments, retirement, and college for your children, vacations, or donations.

LESS INSURANCE

Insurance for your home can add up quickly, especially when it comes time to use it. Tiny houses cost much less to insure because they are less valuable. Many insurance companies consider tiny houses on wheels to be an RV.

Since insurance companies aren't nonprofits and are in business to make money, you will often have difficulty getting the money from them. By owning a tiny house you can minimize the amount you give to them in the first place.

LESS INTEREST PAID

When I bought my first house, initially I was paying more towards interest than the principle. It's no secret that over the course of a 30 year loan, you will pay more for interest than you will the house itself. Most tiny house owners elect to pay cash for their tiny house, or to pay it off quickly.

The amount you save by avoiding interest will ultimately be a huge amount. More than enough to buy the in-laws a tiny house and have it located on the back (way back) of your property.

MORE DISPOSABLE INCOME

All of the above reasons I've listed for buying a tiny house have been focused on "less". Less consumption, less money out of pocket. All of this leads to having more money in the bank at your disposal.

If you write a list of your recurring expenses, you'll quickly realize that costs associated with your home represent the majority of your expenses. By owning and living in a tiny house, you are slashing your living expenses at every level.

MORE FREEDOM

When you own and live in a small house, you free up your two most precious resources, money and time, not to mention some of Earth's most precious resources...water and energy.

By living in a tiny house, you free up money by cutting expenses in a big way. You use less natural resources. You free up time by spending less of it cleaning and maintaining your home. You trade square feet for freedom.

CHAPTER 4
GUIDE TO BUILDING A TINY HOUSE

There are a number of ways to design small house plans to maximize the amount of space available. These approaches are particularly important in urban areas where space is very limited. Most architects who design plans for small houses know the tricks of the trade needed to make the rooms and space look larger.

However, a homeowner should also be educated on the different approaches and techniques for the interior design to make the best use of their tiny house plans.

A common characteristic of small house plans is an attempt to make the room seem like it is bigger than the actual footage of the room. One of the ways architects compensate for the square footage in small home plans is to build high ceilings, thereby making the space feel larger regardless of the actual square footage.

There a number of design tools a homeowner can apply to accent this feature. The owner can create a horizontal border across the room and paint the lower half a slightly darker color and top half a lighter color. This creates a visual illusion of more height.

Homeowners can also compliment their small home plans by buying small paintings that are similar in size and hang them in a vertical line in a prominent area on the wall. This also creates an illusion and draws the focus to the vertical height rather than the length or width.

Another facet homeowners must consider when deciding how to use their small house plans is the placement of furniture. A common mistake made by interior designers for small house plans is using large furniture that does not fit the space.

A huge, overstuffed couch may be a beautiful piece, however in a small space it becomes overbearing. It is important to understand about these plans that every inch is important.

Homeowners must avoid over decorating the rooms to compensate for the size, as the over decorating can emphasize the smallness of the area. The best approach to design for tiny house plans is to keep the furniture and decorations minimal.

The furniture should also range in height. A large lamppost next to the couch will make the couch look less cumbersome. Instead of a heavy bookcase that takes up space, homeowners should use shelves for their books that vary in height, thus saving space and creating a visual illusion

The green-house effect is everywhere these days. You just can't escape the news about how important it is to save energy with efficient appliances and a house that is well insulated-and that's a good thing. But the simplest and most effective way to reduce a home's energy usage in the long run is to reduce its size from the outset.

A shrinking energy bill is just for starters: The need for fewer building materials, less land, and less maintenance is a significant by-product of building smaller houses.

More and more of my clients ask whether a small house can work for them. They're concerned that it won't have enough room for family and friends on holiday visits or that it will just seem cramped.

The reality is that a small house doesn't have to appear nor feel small. By using thoughtful and innovative design techniques, a small house can be made to seem larger and more gracious than its actual dimensions.

On these pages are ten guidelines that can be used to expand the perceived size of a small house. They comprise an overall approach that will yield a house that is both practical and excellent.

To be successful, a small house also should be straightforward, with simple architectural forms and construction techniques, quality materials, and careful detailing. Quality feels better than quantity, while spirit and personality bring a house alive.

1. DESIGN AN OUTDOOR ROOM

What you build outside the house can have a major impact on the way your home feels inside, especially if you make a roomlike space and connect it properly to the house. This outdoor space should have a definite boundary such as a stone wall, a fence, shrubs, a deck railing, or adjacent structures.

It needs to be easily accessible from inside the house and to be linked to the interior by consistent materials, floor patterns, overhangs, plantings, and large doors and/or windows. An element such as an outdoor fireplace or an arrangement of table and chairs also can give this space an interior connection.

The outdoor room should be a bit bigger than the largest room in the house. I typically like to use spaces that are about 1 1/4 to 1 1/2 times as big as the largest room. Ideally, the outdoor room should have an area that is hidden from view, creating a bit of mystery and tempting a visitor to explore. Leave guests with a sense that there is something more to discover.

2. INVEST SOME SPACE IN TRANSITIONS

By using transitions, you can emphasize distinct realms in a house. Transitions range from portions of the floor plan such as stairs, hallways, and balconies, to details such as thick thresholds, substantial columns, overhead beams, and lowered ceilings.

You can use these architectural elements to create a sense of mystery and a process of controlled discovery, enhancing the sense that there is more to the house than immediately meets the eye.

Although it might be tempting to remove square footage from entry and circulation spaces, it is more important to be generous with these areas. Doing so will create the sense that you are living in a bigger house.

3. USE CONTRASTS IN LIGHT AND COLOR

Natural light is a wonderful way to enhance a sense of spaciousness. Bring light into the house by using large windows, skylights, and clerestories. Interior spaces without exterior walls can borrow light from other areas via transoms, French doors, or interior windows.

Bright light in the foreground with slightly darker areas in the background creates a perspective that increases the perceived depth of a space. Light brought into the ends of a room or house attracts the viewer's eye, increasing the perceived distance. A window at the end of a hall or a skylight at the top of the stairs fosters a sense that the space extends farther than its actual size otherwise would suggest.

Artificial lighting also can be used to brighten a room and to illuminate features and tasks. Well-placed lighting provides contrast and shadow, gives definition and clarity to elements and edges, and influences the perception that the space is larger than it actually is.

Although the color scheme should be kept simple, the use of contrasting colors can help to create a sense of expanded space. Light colors on ceilings and walls dissolve the boundaries of a space, making it seem larger; darker colors, on the other hand, enclose the volume of a room, making it feel smaller and more intimate.

Warm colors seem to advance toward us, while cool colors tend to recede. Using color in creative ways can really open up smaller spaces visually.

4. CREATE CONTRAST WITH SCALE

Avoid downsizing everything in a small house, because doing so just makes it feel small. Instead, vary the scale of objects and elements from larger than normal to smaller than normal to evoke a sense of grandeur. For example, a tiny window placed next to a big piece of furniture makes the area seem larger.

Using elements that are monumental can achieve the same effect. A huge fireplace, a grand chimney, an oversize window, a massive door, giant columns, an overstuffed chair, and a formal garden all appear as if they belong to a "greater" house.

Combining large pieces of comfortable furniture with large area rugs is another good idea; you just need to use fewer pieces. Raising the ceiling height from the standard 8 ft. to 9 ft. in the main living areas also can make a big impact.

5. ORGANIZE THE HOUSE INTO DISTINCT ZONES

If you clearly distinguish different areas within a small house, you can make it seem larger by creating the impression that it contains multiple rooms and spatial domains. Establish at least two realms; avoid making a one-room house, unless that is your intention.

Creating public and private zones, separating competing functions, and making distinctions between quiet and noisy areas are all good ways to enlarge the perceived size of a small house. Use well-articulated transitions such as floor-level changes and variable ceiling heights to define and separate different areas.

Contrast spaces by making some of them intimate and snug, and others open and airy. A sheltered inglenook off an open living area is a good example of this tactic.

A "getaway" space somewhere in the house also is important. A small house feels larger and more balanced if you know that it contains a secluded place for quiet and inward-focused activities.

6. DEVELOP MULTIPLE ORIENTATIONS

By creating multiple views with different-size openings, you can enrich a small home's sense of spatial variety. Use windows to frame a view, and vary the focus from nearby features to distant horizons whenever possible. You also can use a mirror to reflect an outdoor view.

Try to give each space natural light from at least two sides. Think of using volume and not just area. For example, a skylight or a high window can open up a cramped interior space and transform it into a bright, airy realm.

Avoid using large areas of glass in small rooms and large windows on only one wall. Doing so can create an uneasy imbalance that sucks the sense of enclosure out of the room, causing it to feel small and separated from the rest of the house.

7. ACCENTUATE THE DIMENSIONS

Start by using sightlines to their full potential. Long hallways strategically placed, one-and-a-half- or two-story spaces, and diagonal views are all ways to gain a sense of spaciousness.

Instead of a solid wall that limits a potential long view, use interior windows, transoms, and clerestories to maximize sightlines and to extend space beyond its perceived boundaries.

Keeping sightlines clear is important. Limit the number of furniture pieces and eliminate clutter in these areas to allow the eye to travel farther, extending perceived spatial dimensions.

8. PUT ILLUSION TO WORK

You can combine tapered walls and ceilings and manipulate the scale of objects such as fireplaces, sculptures, and landscaping to create the illusion of expanded space. For example, an outdoor room with walls that taper toward one another creates a forced perspective that funnels the eye toward a focal point that seems more distant.

Placed at that focal point, an object such as a small sculpture helps to enhance this perception of expanded space.

Another technique is to create a seductive curve by designing a space that beckons visitors into an area partly hidden from view. A curved or angled wall, a loft space, or stairs going up or down can help to create a sense of mystery.

Large mirrors set on closet or bathroom doors and in small rooms can enlarge the perceived space. Be careful to avoid placing mirrors facing each other, however. This arrangement can create a disorienting fun-house effect of endlessly duplicated images.

When deciding how big a mirror should be and where it should go, think of it like a window, a piece of artwork, or a framed picture. Paintings and photographs also can create the illusion of more space when they're placed strategically in a room or at the end of a hallway or staircase.

9. USE THICK EDGES AND BUILT-INS

Thick countertops, deep window jambs, and wide door thresholds are all examples of thick edges. They give the impression of strength and longevity, and express a sense of grandeur.

When you extend a window beyond the exterior plane of a wall, you create thickness around the interior of the window. Inside, the wide jambs reflect light, brightening the room. Outside, shadows cast by the window bay add interest to the facade of the house. Recessing an entry door, on the other hand, lets you create the illusion of a thick wall.

By incorporating thick edges and built-in furniture around the perimeter of a room, the center of the space becomes liberated for living. Built-in furniture such as window seats, wall beds, Pullman bunks, booth seating, and fold-up tables can be used to keep spaces clear of furniture.

Nothing creates a sense of claustrophobia in a small house faster than clutter. Use bookshelves, cupboards, cabinets, drawers, and storage chests to keep clutter out of sight.

Often, nooks and crannies present themselves during remodeling or construction. Think like a boat designer and look for these opportunities to provide places for stowing items away.

10. INCLUDE MULTIPURPOSE ROOMS

Houses integrate numerous functions that don't need their own space all the time. If you can combine different activities that occur at different times into the same space, you can eliminate the need for more rooms.

But don't force it. Work through the functional requirements of different activities before you start to combine them. Here are some typical uses that can double or triple up:

- Hall with laundry and storage
- Bathroom/laundry room
- Entry with bench, storage and powder room
- Mudroom with workbench, sink, and clothes-drying racks
- Bedroom with a comfortable area for reading or meditation
- Stair landing expanded to include a desk
- Dining area that serves both formal and informal dining

CHAPTER 5
HOW TO BUY A TINY HOUSE

Planning is a small word that entails big thinking and brainstorming.

For starters, take a look at many of the details that cannot be forgotten as this project unfolds. Below is a list of the very first items to keep in mind and that will assist in planning ahead. In the meantime, printing this list is a tool that will assist while working.

If you have experience with using an excel program, you'll be able to make a couple of columns; one to have your description and the second one to have your cost estimate for each item.

Another easy and quick way is to prepare it by using a regular paper pad. So go ahead and prepare to plan with this first part of organizing your ideas and putting them into effect.

IDENTIFY YOUR NEEDS

Have you chosen a land, a town, a state for your small house?

Make a sketch of your "would like to have" floor plan or visit pre-fab buildings to picture yourself living inside.

START LOOKING INTO APPROXIMATE PRICES OF APPLIANCES ONLINE TO PREPARE A REALITY BUDGET

a) Refrigerator

b) Stove with or without oven

c) Microwave

d) Toilet (compost, dry water, traditional)

e) Shower station or tub

f) Kitchen and bathroom sink

g) Power source, electric, gas or solar

h) lighting - interior and exterior

LOOK INTO PRICES FOR FURNITURE NEEDED, PRETEND YOU ARE ALREADY LIVING THERE.

a) Love seat, sofa or futon with storage drawers underneath

b) End Table with storage

c) Ottoman with storage

d) Murphy bed, credenza with bed, custom bed that slide under lifted kitchen floor

e) Floating desk, corner desk, drop leaf table, fold away table

f) Coffee table with storage

g) Storage trunks

h) Folding chairs

i) Storage baskets or bins

AFTER YOU HAVE DETERMINED THE SIZE OF YOUR TINY HOUSE, LOOK FOR PRICES ON MATERIALS NEEDED TO BUILD IF YOU HAVE DECIDED TO DO SO.

a) Trailer

b) Windows

c) Lumber, Roofing

d) Plumbing

e) Electrical outlets

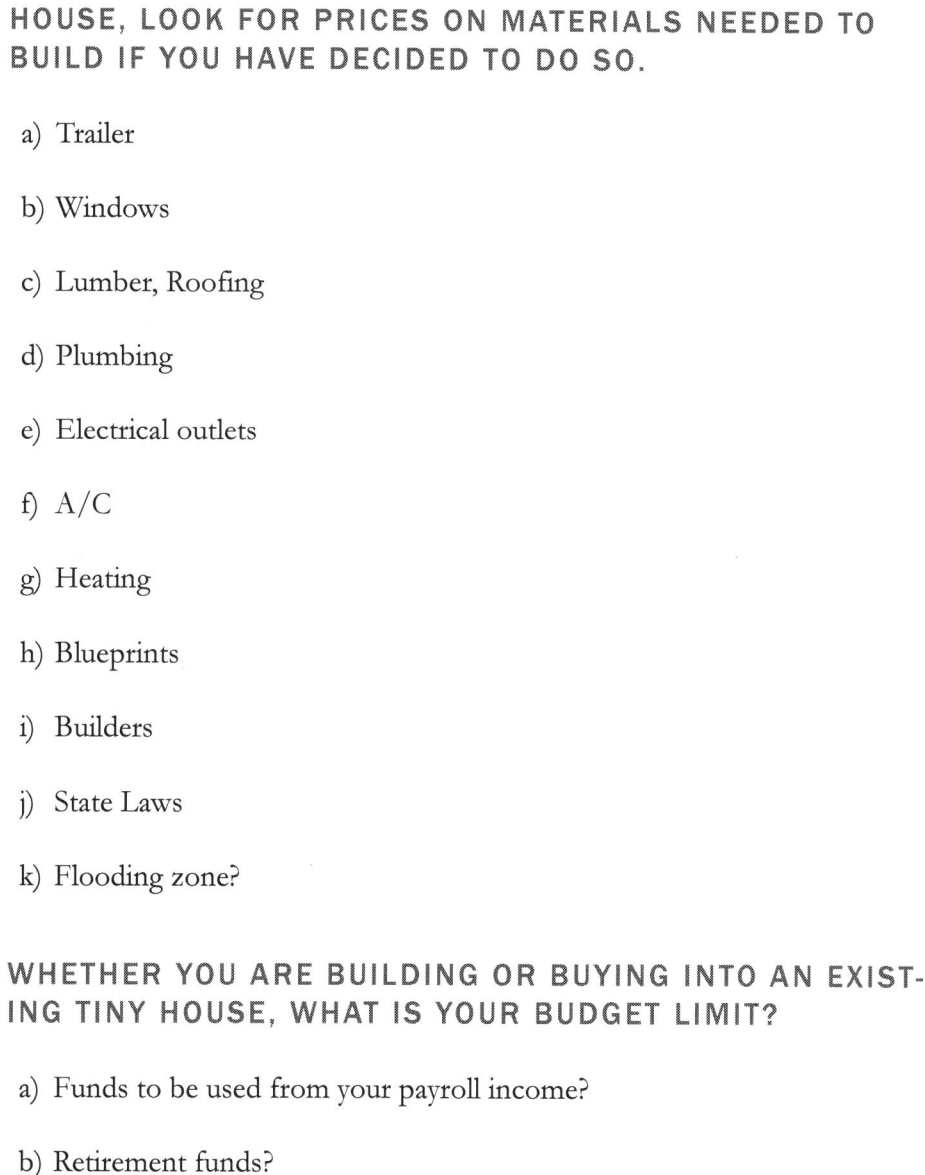

f) A/C

g) Heating

h) Blueprints

i) Builders

j) State Laws

k) Flooding zone?

WHETHER YOU ARE BUILDING OR BUYING INTO AN EXISTING TINY HOUSE, WHAT IS YOUR BUDGET LIMIT?

a) Funds to be used from your payroll income?

b) Retirement funds?

c) Savings?

d) Inheritance?

e) Real Estate sale?

TINY HOUSE COST VS TRADITIONAL HOUSE COST

There are lots of benefits from buying and living in a tiny house. The most obvious is the cost of the home itself.

The issue of land is purposefully excluded since many tiny home owners select to park their homes in a friend's back yard, lease the land, travel, or some similar arrangement. For small homes that are fixed and must have land purchased with them, you would need to take the price of land into consideration.

So, the savings from purchasing a small home are still very substantial. This is just basic information to prove a basic point.

The below numbers show the an approximate average price of a home, the interest paid and the total of both the home cost and the interest paid. The numbers also shows the same for a tiny dwelling.

Although I don't have statistics on the average price of a tiny house, based on my observation I would say the median price is somewhere around $25,000. Some cost less and some that come with all of the bells and whistles cost more.

The numbers also shows the interest paid on a 30 year note for a traditional house, and a 15 year note for a tiny house at 4.5% interest.

HOW MUCH CAN BE SAVED BY PURCHASING A TINY HOME?

COST OF THE HOUSE

Traditional house = $156,100

Tiny house = $25,00

Interest Paid

Traditional house (30 year loan) = $128,636.87

Tiny house (15 year loan) = $9,424.70

Total Paid (cost + interest)

Traditional house = $284.736.87

Tiny House = $34,424.70

This means that the cost of a tiny home only represents approximately 12% of the cost of an average traditional home.

A typical American family's rent or mortgage payment represents roughly 30% of their total income. This is before they put a piece of bread on the table or pay their utilities.

If a potential home buyer bought a tiny home and gave up the extra square footage of a traditional home, they could quickly pay off their home and could focus their financial efforts elsewhere, such as retirement, vacations, changing careers, more time with their family, and so on.

CHAPTER 6
SPACE SAVING HACKS AND FURNITURE

First of all, we must keep in mind to plan for the needs as well as the extra comfort we are all used to. For instance, how about planning to have that dream pantry slide-out within the kitchen area or near?

We are willing to downsize, however, why not do it smartly! Here are many options to keep within your planning:

- over-the-door organizer baskets for the bathroom
- jewelry and makeup storage cabinet that closes and brings a mirror when closed
- love seats with storage underneath
- sofa/futons that bring drawers
- ottomans with spacious storage
- small home office storage ottomans
- benches with storage
- over-the-door shoe organizers
- folding tables
- drop leaf tables

- floating desks

- folding chairs

- wall mounted beds

- credenza hide away beds

- lift up beds with storage underneath

- over the toilet organizing cabinet

- small corner cabinets

- storage baskets or bins

- sleeper chairs that fold out

Second, if you plan to have a loft but find it too tight to sleep up there, instead think about using it as extra storage space by using large plastic containers for out of season clothing, sports or camping gear. It can also serve the double duty of an office space, as while you are sitting down working on a desk, your head space should be adequate.

Installing a wall bed on the first floor will provide more comfort and is a space saving idea as well. Some wall beds bring a desk underneath and used while the bed is hidden up against the wall. This table or desk will could also be used for meals. Think big when you decide to live tiny.

Other tiny house interiors can be made with a lifted kitchen floor. If your tiny house is 8' ft wide, then an option is to construct 3 steps that measure approximately 2' ft. Wide on one side, and the other side can have a roll out bed underneath the lifted kitchen floor.

The bed measures approximately 6 ft. Wide for a double or queen size bed. How smart is that? When you slide out the bed half-way... You may also use it as your sitting area.

How about a bed that has an electrical mechanism that slides up into the ceiling or down for sleeping? As said by Plato, "necessity is the mother of invention". Get creative by inviting family and friends to brainstorm with you as you plan your future tiny dream home.

Lastly, many more innovative ideas will be born as you brainstorm and plan your tiny house interior for your new lifestyle.

CHAPTER 7
THINGS TO CONSIDER WHEN BUYING TINY HOUSE KITS

Purchasing the appropriate tiny house kits doesn't have to be major hurdle and one has a lot of reasons why they are better off buying one. It is the more convenient and cost effective option in building your dream lodge.

However, before immediately buying the first one that comes around, it is essential that you do your research and consider all the available choice so that you will find the unit that fits your lifestyle and preferences.

It is also important that you learn some important things about log cottages and their essential components such as cabin windows, doors, etc. so that you are able to weigh your options and make an informed decision.

When you choose lodging assembly sets you are going for an option that has a proven track record and a checkered history. Log cottages were the preferred building method in the past and were commonly used in Scandinavia, Russia and other parts of Eastern Europe.

This home building concept was brought to America by the Scandinavian immigrants in the 17th century. Up until the early 19th century, most of the lodges were made out of hand-hewn timber and after a few years, milled logs were gradually introduced.

At present, when you are buying log sets you must have to consider many things before making your final decision. One of the major considerations when deciding on the most appropriate lodge assembly sets is your preferred log type.

Majority of the log sets that are available in the market today are either machine-profiled or milled logs although there are still those that are made of logs that are handcrafted. One of the main advantages of logs that are machine-profiled is that these are more convenient and simpler to use.

Because of this, the log cottage sets that use milled logs are more expensive. One can also explore other options that are available when you opt for logs that are machine-profiled and all these options have lesser workload.

One must understand that there are still other things to consider once you opt for the use of machine-profiled timber. There are different processing methods of milled timber and your choice will depend largely on the quality that you require from the log material that you are going to use in building your dream cottage.

The assembly sets will also include all the essential components and accessories needed to complete the construction of your dream chalet. These include the doors, porches as well as other parts which the clients want in their cottage.

One of the most effective ways of familiarizing yourself with all the critical aspects about log cottages is by researching online. You can find useful information and leads to practical and best offers by checking the Websites of manufacturers and suppliers of log cottage assembly sets. In this way, you are able to broaden your options.

Before making your final decision, it is important that you make an ocular inspection of your short listed choices and see for yourself how each of these choices fit your lifestyle and preference.

CHAPTER 8
TINY HOUSE PLANS

Keep in mind the width of your entry door for appliances, bathroom shower, tub and toilet, furniture and mattress in order to avoid surprises. Can you imagine if one of your most important things on your "want and need" list didn't fit through? Make plans by measuring for small space furniture also.

AND WHAT ABOUT BUYING A TRAILER FOR YOUR TINY HOUSE. HERE ARE A FEW STEPS THAT WILL HELP YOU TO PLAN SOME MORE PRIOR TO STARTING:

Trailer - Is it the length and width I need?

Do you have a site?

Do I have to level out the land?

If an existing Tiny House, are there any decks to be removed for relocating?

Do I need anchors?

Do I need to build a foundation?

Do you have blueprints/plans and a builder?

Other recommendations to have in mind are to speak to other tiny house owners, attend workshops and even subscribe to tiny house newsletters for further information. Have you seen construction plans and know what you would like to live in? Some sites have the entire building plans that include electrical and plumbing.

Having communication, chatting and blogging with sites like these will open your eyes into many things, that otherwise you wouldn't have thought of. For example, one of the newsletters was mind opening to see a bed slide out from a risen kitchen floor.

The kitchen floor was about 3 steps up, the left hand side had the hidden bed underneath the floor and on the right hand side is where they placed the 3 steps to access the kitchen. How cool is this idea? Never would have crossed my mind as lofts is what you usually find in a tiny house.

TOOLS:

- Air Compressor
- Measuring Tape
- Hammer
- Impact Driver
- Nail Gun
- Electric Drill
- Circular and Jig Saws
- Table
- Carpenter's Square
- Level
- Wall framing

- Windows (style, quantity and size)

- Skylight (style, quantity and size)

- Doors (style, quantity and size)

- Hardware (bits, nuts, nails, staples, misc.)

- Roofing (type)

- Sidings (type)

- Exterior Trim Work (style)

- Gas Lines if needed

- Electrical (outlets, lighting)

- Heating

- Plumbing (faucets, toilet, shower, sinks)

- Insulation

- Flooring (style, type)

By now you will find yourself deep into commitment and really looking forward to the outcome of all your planning and hard work. Now that we are sure everything fits through the main door, it's almost time to relax with pride. Everyone involved in making the dream come true will be experiencing the satisfaction of hard and intelligent work.

CHAPTER 9
TINY HOMES FAQS

Historically, periods of economic hardship have resulted in success stories for large and small corporations alike. Companies that offer tiny houses may be the next great success stories on the "timeline" of our country. Without a doubt, this concept offers great spaces in great places.

These homes are a creative and innovative alternative to traditional home ownership amidst a changed economic climate and a distressed housing market. Tiny houses offer alternatives to paying high rent and are portable which alleviates the red tape of building codes and permits.

Tiny houses are generally built to include 50 to 750 square feet and come complete with all of the necessary features of a comfortable home including portable heating and air conditioning.

Thanks to portable climate control, homeowners of tiny houses can even have outdoor pet houses and not have to worry about their pets acquiring heat or cold related illnesses.

Tiny homes do not have unused hallway spaces and promote a more "Earth Friendly" lifestyle. Tiny houses are also a great option for those who may be seeking a cabin or a "second home" away from the hustle and bustle of life.

Hallways in tiny houses can be utilized for storage spaces and homes are complete with a designer feel and look much like modern day homes. The benefits of living in tiny houses are numerous and include:

- No or low mortgage payments

- A significant decrease in monthly utility bills

- The possibility of "off-grid" living

- More choices in where a person would like to live (think rural versus urban)

- Feeling a greater sense of control over one's finances, regardless of what's happening on the "national/global" scene

- The ability to add a rental property for additional income for a fraction of the cost of new building construction

- A lifestyle based upon simplicity, rather than complexity

After giving the "tiny house" concept some consideration, many may ponder this question "if my home is smaller, if I have less material items, can my house still be a home?" Is "keeping up with the Joneses" more important than focusing on our passions and dreams?

CHAPTER 10
HOW TO MAKE IT BIG WITH TINY HOUSE KITS

With the emergence of advanced building systems and ready access to cranes and other heavy equipment, tiny cabin homes are becoming a popular choice both in the rural and suburban settings. These easy to assemble small log homes are pre-processed logs and usually come as tiny house kits.

The logs are the predominant feature of the exterior as well as the interior of the tiny home structure. The log cabin kit follows a carefully developed template for an ideal rustic design complete with the requisite cabin windows, doors and even partitions.

For most of us who want to have a log cabin for functional reasons or even as an addition to your home property must seriously consider the small cabin kit.

If you want to go through the trouble in your dealings with the architect, construction specialist, carpenter, plumber and other professionals to complete your small home construction or improvement project then buying a small cabin kit is your best alternative.

Once you already made up your mind to start with the project, the first thing that you have to firm up is your budget for the project.

You have to make a list of all the essential services that you will require in completing your project. Before you start the project, finalize how you are going to finance your project. Are you going to utilize your equity or are you going to seek financing for your project.

You also must meet all the State documentary requirements and other requisites for the construction of the small log cabin kits. Make sure you are able to get the appropriate building permit and pass the building inspection requirements of the state or county.

Once you are done with the preliminaries, you are all set to start the construction phase of your home construction or home improvement project. The initial concerns that have to be immediately addressed are the cooling and heating system for your small house.

The log cabin kits are provided with furnaces and wood burning stoves which are used to for the cooling requirements of your log structure. The later version of wood burning techniques is basically cost effective, efficient and practical to use.

Once you decide on this kind of heating and cooling facility then it is important for you to carefully route the chimney of your functional home. You can also explore other heating and cooling alternatives and make your final decision based on the overall design and the available budget.

The next one that needs your decision shall be the location. The location and size will be affected to a large extent by the constraints that are brought upon us by the specific log cabin kit. You will also have to decide based on the accessibility to utilities such as power and water.

Once you are able to pinpoint the exact location where you are going to site the log cabin, then you are ready to finally search for the most appropriate and functional small log cabin kits. There are considerable numbers of home developers who are exclusively carrying small log cabin assembly kits.

You can ask from the dealer or the construction options for practical and professional ideas which you can adopt once you start considering the design of your small log cabin. You may also opt for a customized log cabin.

CHAPTER 11
THE ADVANTAGES OF LIVING IN TINY HOUSES

Recent economic difficulties have forced everyone to make some hard choices when it comes to the household budget. Many people are downsizing everything in their lives from the cars they drive to the homes they live in.

For some, the movement toward tiny houses is about saving money but for others, the opportunity to live a simpler life is just as big a draw.

The average size of a tiny house is between 100 square feet and 400 square feet. By comparison, the average size of new houses built in the United States in 2013 was approximately 2,600 square feet. A compact living space is attractive to individuals of all ages, including college graduates, newlyweds, and retirees.

One of the most obvious advantages of a home this small is the owner does not need a huge plot of land. The house is portable enough to move virtually anywhere. Manufacturing costs are low because builders do not need as much material and it takes fewer hours to assemble.

That translates in a significantly smaller price tag making it affordable to more consumers. Tiny house owners do not have to worry about signing a 30-year mortgage just to have a roof over their heads.

The savings continue long after moving into this type of house. They are much less expensive to heat and cool than a house that covers a couple thousand square feet. Miniaturized appliances cost less to purchase and require fewer resources to operate.

New construction traditionally puts a strain on the Earth's natural resources. Moving into a tiny house is especially attractive to those people who want to reduce their carbon footprint. Because of their size, many of these homes are constructed with recycled materials. After they are built, they are energy efficient and produce less waste.

Tiny house designs make the maximum use of the space available. Concealed storage closets and cubbyholes take advantage of areas that are typically wasted. Without extra space, occupants are less inclined to accumulate possessions that they do not really need.

Without the clutter, the rooms appear and feel bigger than they actually are. Cutting down on purchasing impulse items means less waste, less money spent, and more money saved.

Many people realize that they lead a higher quality of life after they have eliminated unnecessary possessions. They lose the desire to buy status items just to keep up with their peers. They feel less stressed and receive more happiness out of the little things in life that are more important in the grand scheme of things.

A smaller home means less time spent on maintenance and cleaning. Instead of taking hours to dust, vacuum, and wash windows, it takes just a few minutes to clean the entire house from top to bottom. This means more time spent with family and enjoying life.

Despite all the benefits, living this type of lifestyle is not for every. Before making the commitment to living in a tiny home, individuals should weigh their options and consider the disadvantages of downsizing to just a few hundred square feet of living space.

One of the biggest problems is likely to be deciding which possessions to keep and which to sell, donate, or discard. As difficult as it may be, many people find this process to be liberating once they make it through.

Living in smaller quarters requires a high level of organization. A little bit of clutter goes a long way in a small space. Someone who cannot stay organized will become quickly overwhelmed. The home will look more like a storage closet and will lose all of its appeal.

Someone who loves to entertain guests at home will have a hard time following this lifestyle. Accommodating any extra people indoors will be challenging if not impossible. Depending on the climate and the time of year, homeowners can consider entertaining guests outdoors.

Creative use of outdoor space is an effective way to increase the amount of usable space available. A porch or deck provides a comfortable place to barbecue, dine, or just kick back and relax whenever the weather permits.

The reasons people choose to move to smaller homes are personal but many are looking for a simple life and a way to escape living from paycheck to paycheck. The satisfaction of being self-sufficient is something else that people gain when they downsize their living space.

Moving into a tiny home can be the ideal solution for someone who wants to achieve financial freedom while living a lifestyle that is friendly to the environment.

CONCLUSION

Tiny houses are becoming more and more desirable. Not only are these houses more financially manageable for many, but the appeal they offer goes beyond just finances. Many Americans are looking for a simpler life.

Many of us are realizing that life is not all about our possessions-there more to it than the material objects you can call your own. We are, possibly, on the track to becoming minimalists.

Well, at least some of us are. I like my home and I like the space it gives me. I don't think I could live in a space consisting of less than 100 square feet. No, I definitely couldn't. But some people can.

Whether or not you think you're one of the people who could live in such a small place, and live in it happily, is not really the point here. The point is, we are all, as a people, heading in a hopeful direction.

I feel that this change of heart, or change of perspective, is a good thing and a hopeful thing. I feel that it's a positive thing. And even though I may never be the type to downsize to a tiny home, I think I'm on track to being the type of person who can say to myself, "Just because you have the space, doesn't mean you need to fill the space."

I encourage you all to take a look around and really ask yourself how many of your beloved possessions you really, really need. There could be someone else out there who could need them more. And during the holiday season especially, there are plenty of open hands willing to accept your "stuff".

TRY A TINY HOUSE TODAY!

Printed in Great Britain
by Amazon